PRESENTED TO

_____

BY

_____

True friends are a sure refuge.

ARISTOTLE

The TREASURE

JOHN C. MAXWELL AND
DAN REILAND

o f a FRIEND

J. COUNTRYMAN *Nashville, Tennesee*

Copyright © 1999 by INJOY Ministries, Norcross, Georgia 30092

Published by J. Countryman®, a division of Thomas Nelson, Inc.,
Nashville, Tennessee 37214

Project editor—Jenny Baumgartner

Designed by David Uttley Design, Sisters, Oregon

ISBN 0-8499-5506-8

Published in association with Sealy M. Yates, Literary Agent, Orange
County, California

Printed and bound in the United States of America

n December 18, 1998, I suffered a serious heart attack. At the time, I thought I wasn't going to make it. My doctors later told me that if I'd experienced the attack four years ago, it would have killed me because before my attack, they didn't have the technology that saved my life.

I look back on that day now, and I thank God for many things. First I thank Him for life. And I am grateful that I didn't suffer any permanent heart damage. But I also appreciate the circumstances surrounding my heart attack. You see, it happened during the Christmas party for my company, The INJOY Group. And because of that, my wife, children, and closest friends were all there. In what I expected were the last moments of my life, I was with the people who mattered most to me. I was able to tell them how much I love them.

You see, every now and then I think we need to be reminded of the treasures we have around us. That's why my friend Dan Reiland, who was one of the people with me that night, and I wrote this book. We want to help you recognize the treasures you have in your life—and be able to do it without the heart attack!

Read this book and thank God for the friends He's given you. And if you received this book as a gift, know that your friend appreciates you as the treasure you are.

JOHN C. MAXWELL

SEPTEMBER 1999

The
TREASURE
of a
FRIEND

A single real friend is a treasure
worth more than gold or precious stones.

C. D. PRENTICE

A
TRUE FRIEND

True friendship . . .
is infinite and immortal.

PLATO

My friends have made the story of my life.
In a thousand ways they have turned my limitations into
beautiful privileges, and enabled me to walk serene and
happy in the shadow cast by my deprivation.

HELEN KELLER

PRAYING HANDS

As children, brothers Hans and Albrecht, the German-born sons of a Hungarian goldsmith, dreamt about becoming great artists. And they both began studying art at an early age. But times were difficult for their family in the late 1400s, and it soon became clear that their studies were a luxury the family could not afford. It looked like the brothers would have to return to their father's shop and become goldsmiths.

But that disturbed Hans. He saw that his brother had a great gift for artistry, and he didn't want that wonderful talent to be wasted. Thus, Hans gave himself to the family trade so that Albrecht could continue studying.

And study he did. Apprenticing under painter and printer Michael Wolgemut, he blossomed into a profoundly talented artist. Many consider Albrecht Dürer the greatest German artist of the Renaissance era. He went on to create world-famous prints, such as

The Four Horsemen of the Apocalypse, The Passion of Christ, and *The Last Supper.*

Though not Dürer's most dramatic or spectacular work, *Study of Praying Hands* is one of his most poignant pieces. It displays the sinewy, callused hands of a laborer coming together in the contrite act of prayer. It embodies the humble dependence on God believers are to possess. Who was the model for Albrecht Dürer's famous work? None other than his brother Hans, the man who made it possible for him to pursue his calling as an artist. For all time, this expression of Dürer's faith also symbolizes the deep love, appreciation, and friendship of one brother for another.

THE UNSHAKABLE COMPANION

A friend loves at all times,
and a brother is born for adversity.

PROVERBS 17:17 (NKJV)

Being a friend is easy when times are good
or when you benefit from the relationship.
But a true friend sticks by your side even
when things get tough. This is the kind of
friend you desire. But to have one, this is
also the kind of friend you must be.

The only way to have a friend is to be one.

RALPH WALDO EMERSON

LOVE AND FRIENDSHIP

Love is still the greatest cure the world has ever known—
no matter what the problem. The love of a friend makes
you feel totally accepted, just the way you are. The love
of a friend asks how you are and really listens for an
answer. The love of a friend touches you—even though
she knows all about you, she loves you anyway. The love
of a friend stays with you when others desert you. The
love of a friend is a gift from God.

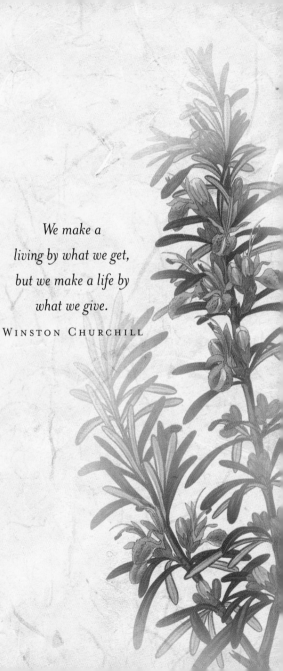

*We make a
living by what we get,
but we make a life by
what we give.*

WINSTON CHURCHILL

Friendship is unnecessary, like philosophy, like art . . .
It has not survival value; rather it is one of those
things that gives value to survival.

C. S. LEWIS

My only sketch, profile, of Heaven is a large blue sky . . .
larger than the biggest I have seen in June—
and in it are my friends—every one of them.

EMILY DICKINSON

FRIENDS WHO GO
THE DISTANCE

inishing a marathon is no small feat. It's something few people ever achieve. But it's one thing to complete a marathon and another to try to improve your time in a 26.6 mile race. But that was Mark's goal.

Breaking the three-hour-and-thirty-minute barrier was his objective. Now, to a world-class marathon racer, that may not sound like much—the world record stands at under two hours and ten minutes—but it was a great challenge for Mark. He had tried to beat his personal best many times before and failed. If he didn't do it this time, he decided that he never would, because this would be his last try.

He trained all summer for the race. It was difficult to tell which was worse—the running itself, the countless hours he invested, or the oppressive midsummer heat.

But Mark was willing to make the sacrifices, and as the race approached, he felt that he was as ready as he could be.

He also had a race-day strategy that would help him. His father, father-in-law, and wife Valerie would be riding alongside him on bicycles, encouraging him every mile. More importantly, Valerie would try to keep him on track with a pacing chart he had created. He also planned to have his buddy Don meet him at the twenty-five-mile mark so that they could run the last part of the race together.

The race began without a hitch. Mile after mile Mark ran. The first ten miles almost seemed easy. But he had to start pushing himself for the next five. Breathing heavy, his sides hurting, his legs burning, he ran on. Finally he made it to the twenty-mile mark, and still he was on pace.

Somewhere between mile twenty-two and twenty-four, Mark hit "the wall"—the place where a runner's body gives up and only his mind can keep him going.

Most racers begin cataloging reasons they should give up at this point. Many first-time marathoners do. Mark had pushed himself beyond the wall before, so he was in no real danger of giving up. But fatigue was taking its toll. His legs were on fire, his knees were getting wobbly, and the pain was all but unbearable. Mark's support crew kept encouraging him, but the inevitable was happening: He was slowing down. If he stayed at his current pace, he wasn't going to achieve his goal.

When Mark and his crew reached the twenty-five mile mark, Don was there. Don had already run his own race that morning—a half marathon, a distance that was a great challenge for him, and he was exhausted.

As Don stood waiting, his muscles were tightening up. When he saw Valerie, he forced himself to start moving and trotted next to her. "How's he doing?" he asked.

"Not so good, Don," she answered. "He's fifteen seconds behind. I don't think he's going to make it."

Fifteen seconds! That may not sound like much, but it's a huge amount of time for a runner to make up—especially at the end of a marathon. But Don didn't lose hope. He moved up alongside Mark.

"Hey, Buddy. You're almost home," Don said. He smoothed out his stride as he ran. "All right, now. I want you to try to match my stride. Okay?"

Mark just nodded as he kept panting. As he ran, he looked over toward Don, and his steps became more regular.

"That's great," said Don. "Mark, you're a little behind. We're going to pick up the pace a little, okay?" Mark nodded again. His mind was only barely tracking what Don was saying, but he trusted his friend and did what he said.

Side by side they ran. After only a half a mile, Don started hurting, but he knew he couldn't let up. Suddenly, this last mile seemed more important to him than his own race had earlier in the day.

"You're doing great," Don said.

Each step was agony for Mark, but he kept going, listening to his friend. Finally, they could see the finish line ahead. "This is it," Don barked. "Last kick." With the finish in sight, they both gave up their last little bit of energy, and Mark actually finished a half a step ahead of his "coach."

Today Mark looks back at that race with satisfaction. But even stronger is his sense of gratitude. He gives the credit to Don, because without him he never would have broken his personal best—and run the race in 3:29:50.

A genuine friend encourages and challenges
us to live out our best thoughts, honor our purest motives,
and achieve our most significant dreams.

DAN REILAND

CLOSER THAN A BROTHER

*Some friends don't help,
but a true friend is closer than
your own family.*

PROVERBS 18:24 (CEV)

Loyalty is the lifeblood of real friendship. Invest deeply in a few friends rather than superficially among many. Select your friends carefully, and then stick with them.

Oh, the inexpressible comfort
of feeling safe with a person; having neither
to weigh thoughts nor measure words,
but to pour them all out, just as they are,
chaff and grain together,
knowing that a faithful hand will take
and sift them, keep what is worth keeping,
and then, with the breath of kindness,
blow the rest away.

GEORGE ELIOT

The best way to keep
your friendships alive is to bury
the faults of your friends.

UNKNOWN

A Friendship by Any Other Name

o one criticizes the young rose when it's only a small bud and not yet open. It is beautiful right where it is, in the course of its growth. No one points at the thorns and complains that they are sharp and dangerous. No one complains that the rose needs water and sunshine to grow and someone to cultivate the ground. We simply gaze in wonder at its beauty, from bud to full blossom.

The same is true of friendship. Like the rose, it is beautiful in each of its seasons. Don't point out its shortcomings or potential faults. Never focus on its weaknesses. With time, love, nurturing, and faith, friendship will grow. Take time to stop and breathe in its fragrance and appreciate its development.

MEEKNESS

*Finally, all of you should agree
and have concern and love for each other.
You should also be kind and humble.*

1 PETER 3:8 (CEV)

Living in harmony with others is no easy
task. The key is putting others ahead of
yourself. Humility takes the focus off of
you. Compassion helps you refocus it
on someone else. Do that, and you really
can love others as brothers and sisters.

A friend is one who takes me for what I am.

HENRY DAVID THOREAU

LOOKING FOR A FRIEND?

If you don't have many friends, don't fret or have a pity party. Instead of dwelling on what you don't have, think about what you can give. Look for a few people who interest you, begin to communicate that you care in small ways, and invest in their lives. It may begin with something as simple as a word of encouragement. Give them room. If they don't respond, don't force it. And don't sulk. There are hundreds of potential friends out there! Finding the right friend begins with being the right friend.

Nobody cares how much you know—
until they know how much you care.

JOHN CASSIS

FRIENDS TO THE END

Earl C. Willer tells the story of two men who grew up the best of friends. Though Jim was just a little older than Phillip and often assumed the role of leader, they did everything together. They even went to high school and college together.

After college they decided to join the marines. By a unique series of circumstances they were actually sent to Germany together where they fought side by side in one of history's ugliest wars.

One sweltering day during a fierce battle, amid heavy gunfire, bombing, and close-quarters combat, they were given the command to retreat. As the men were running back, Jim noticed that Phillip had not returned with the others. Panic gripped his heart. Jim knew that if Phillip was not back in another minute or two, then he wouldn't make it.

Jim begged his commanding officer to let him

go after his friend, but in an outrage, the officer forbade the request, saying it would be suicide.

Risking his own life, Jim disobeyed and went after Phillip. His heart pounding, praying, and out of breath, he ran into the gunfire, calling out for Phillip. A short time later, his platoon saw him hobbling across the field carrying a limp body in his arms.

Jim's commanding officer upbraided him, shouting that it was a foolish waste of time and an outrageous risk.

"You're friend is dead," he added, "and there was nothing you could do."

"No sir, you're wrong," Jim replied. "You see, I got there just in time. Before he died, his last words were, 'I knew you would come.'"

CARING ENOUGH TO
CONFRONT

A truly good friend will openly correct you.
You can trust a friend who corrects you,
but kisses from an enemy are nothing but lies.

PROVERBS 27:5–6 (CEV)

No one likes to be corrected, but from a loving friend correction can be a great gift. Do you have friends who are living beneath their potential? If you truly care about them, you will confront them in love.

*Happy is the house that
shelters a friend.*

RALPH WALDO EMERSON

OUT OF THE ASHES

hat do you do when your best friend loses everything he owns in a terrible fire? Mark and Pete were trying to come up with an answer to that question when their best friend Devon lost his home in a fire.

The three buddies from Denver had always been inseparable. They graduated from high school together, worked at the YMCA together, and skied, camped, and fished together. They even triple-dated. When Pete lost his dad, Mark and Devon comforted him. And when Mark's grandmother died, the other guys were there for him.

The three young men dreamt of becoming firefighters—together, of course. Devon even played the part by buying a dalmatian he named Captain. Thus, the irony was horrible when Devon, who lived in a fixed-up barn on his parents' property, lost everything to a fire after his wood-burning stove malfunctioned.

But the worst part was that his beloved dog Captain was unable to escape the flames.

Mark and Pete knew they needed to show Devon their support, but the question was *how*. Their friend needed even the most basic things, but items such as food or clothes just didn't seem to communicate what they had in their hearts. But then they had an idea.

The next day the young men showed up at Devon's parents' house with a special gift. As Devon watched, Mark pulled a small, fuzzy, dalmatian puppy from behind his back.

"His name is Phoenix," said Pete, and tears rolled down Devon's cheeks. And similar to the phoenix from mythology, that puppy emerged out of the ashes of Devon's tragedy to ease the pain of his experience. It was a gift from the heart. No other present could have better expressed the bond between the three buddies.

Do not keep the alabaster boxes
of your love and tenderness sealed up
until your friends are dead.
Fill their lives with sweetness.
Speak approvingly cheering words
while their ears can hear them and while
their hearts can be thrilled by them.

GEORGE W. CHILDS

You can always tell a real friend.
When you've made a fool of yourself,
he doesn't feel you've done
a permanent job.

LAWRENCE J. PETER

A FRIEND INDEED

Warm as a crackling fire,

Sweet as hot chocolate,

Comforting as a child's embrace.

Few things are more precious,

Few more cherished,

than the value of a genuine friend.

A friend is a person with whom I may be sincere.

Before him I may think aloud.

RALPH WALDO EMERSON

MEASURE FOR MEASURE

Don't condemn others,
and God won't condemn you. God will be
as hard on you as you are on others!
He will treat you exactly as you treat them.
You can see the speck in your friend's eye,
but you don't notice the log in your own eye.

MATTHEW 7:1–3 (CEV)

Who among us is without blame? It is better to concentrate on the strengths of your friends, rather than on their weaknesses. Instead, focus on the things that need correction in your own life.

WHO ELSE BUT A FRIEND?

To believe in your dreams,

To share your joys,

To dry your tears.

To give you hope,

To comfort your hurts,

To listen.

To laugh with you,

To show you a better way,

To tell you the truth,

To encourage you.

Who else can do that for you?

That's what friends are for.

A joy shared is a joy doubled.

JOHANN WOLFGANG VON GOETHE

A Season to Remember

is name was Andy, but they called him Little Chubby—a nickname that sticks when you're a 5-feet 4-inch ninth grader who weights 185 pounds and looks like he has no knees. Like many kids, Andy dreamed of playing baseball in the big leagues. As a little leaguer in northern Michigan, he imagined that his games were being watched by a professional scout who would someday recruit him for the pros.

The day he joined his high school team, the coach promised that every player would run faster, hit harder, and field better with his help. In fact, he promised every player that he would steal at least one base by the season's end. The boys only needed to hustle and follow what he said.

Andy held onto that promise—at first with great anticipation. But he didn't play much, and as the season wore on, his hope began to fade. By the time the team suited up for the last game, every player on the team had stolen a base but one—you guessed it, Little Chubby.

When the coach signaled him from the dugout to be a pinch runner during the ninth inning, Andy's heart began to race. He knew this was his last chance. As he ran onto the field, he was a little embarrassed because the guys on the bench came to their feet and began to cheer.

He stepped onto first base and took a lead. Then he looked over to his coach who was standing at third. When his coach gave the sign, off Andy went.

As he ran toward second, he gave it everything he had, but he felt like he was moving in quicksand. He just couldn't get his legs to move fast enough. When he felt like he had finally gotten some speed, he could hear his teammates shouting, "Slide, Chubby, Slide!"

It wasn't pretty. He went headfirst, like Pete Rose, but because he started his slide so late and had so much momentum, he slid right over the top of second base and on toward left field. Even though he had beaten the throw from the catcher, he thought he'd blown it. But God was smiling on Andy that day. The catcher's throw was far from the mark, and Andy scrambled back over to the bag. He was safe.

That evening after the game, the coach took the team out for pizza. Based on the way all the players were treating Little Chubby, bystanders at nearby tables probably thought the short, stocky kid had hit the game-winning home run.

Andy felt like a hero. But the real hero was his coach. He had believed in Andy and "made good" on his promise. And even though Andy didn't play all that much or perform all that well, Andy walked away feeling like he'd had a season to remember.

True friends are a sure refuge.

ARISTOTLE

A true friend is one
who hears and understands when you
share your deepest feelings.
He supports you when you are struggling;
he corrects you, gently and with love,
when you err; and he forgives you when you fail.
A true friend prods you to personal growth,
stretches you to your full potential.
And most amazing of all, he celebrates your
successes as if they were his own.

RICHARD EXLEY

Generous Hearts

*Love each other as brothers and sisters
and honor others more than you do
yourself. Never give up. Eagerly follow the
Holy Spirit and serve the Lord. Let your
hope make you glad. Be patient in time of
trouble and never stop praying.
Take care of God's needy people and
welcome strangers into your home.*

Romans 12:10–13 (cev)

Joy and laughter are essential to a
healthy relationship. So is consistency in
sincere prayer and generosity with your
possessions. After all, your friends are
more valuable than anything you own.

Wishing to be friends is quick work,
but friendship is slow–ripening fruit.

ARISTOTLE

What's Worth Carrying to the Ends of the Earth?

I n 1907 British explorer Ernest Henry Shackleton organized the first expedition ever to declare the South Pole as its goal. Shackleton was no stranger to adventure. He had traveled the world since he was sixteen years old, when he was an apprentice in the British Merchant Navy. And his heart for exploration had already taken him to the Antarctic as early as 1901, when he accompanied Robert F. Scott.

Shackleton knew the trip would be daunting, but while he and his companions were in the midst of the journey, conditions became disastrous. The subzero temperatures made the wind-chill factor nearly lethal. Visibility was almost nonexistent, and hope was growing dim. Their bodies ached with fatigue, and every step required incredible effort and tremendous discipline. Then their food ran short. With only ninety-seven nautical miles left to travel to the South Pole, they realized they had to abandon their goal and turn back, which added heartache to their already horrible circumstances.

As they made their desperate return toward safety, they realized they had to discard many items they carried so they could travel lighter. As Shackleton observed what his companions chose to keep and discard, he learned a lot about them. The first thing to go was money. The next was food, despite the shortage. What do you think they kept and cherished most? Pictures of loved ones and letters from home. The love of their families and the hope of seeing them again kept them going. And in the end, it brought them safely home again.

If I don't have friends, then I ain't got nothin'.
BILLIE HOLIDAY

How Do You
Spell Friendship?

Forgive each other.

Refresh each other.

Invest in each other.

Encourage each other.

Nurture each other.

Depend on each other.

Share with each other.

Help each other.

Inspire each other.

Pray for each other.

*If the first law of friendship is that it
has to be cultivated, the second law is to be indulgent
when the first law has been neglected.*

VOLTAIRE

*I am a big believer that you have to
nourish any relationship.
I am still very much a part of my
friends' lives, and they are very
much a part of my life.
A First Lady who does not have this
source of strength and comfort can lose
perspective and become isolated.*

NANCY REAGAN

OPEN ARMS

*But God has combined members of
the body . . . its parts should have
equal concern for each other.*

1 CORINTHIANS 12:24–25 (NIV)

Are you holding something against a
friend? Go and make amends. Whatever
is within your power to resolve, do it.
Confess whatever part of the fault was
yours, no matter how small. And extend
your hand in forgiveness. Friends are
precious gifts from God, not to be set
aside lightly.

The Golden Rule

Treat others
just as you want to be treated.

Luke 6:31 (cev)

The key to friendship is being treated
with kindness, and respect lies in your
willingness to go first—without expecting
anything in return.

One's friends are
that part of the human race with
which one can be human.

George Santayana

JACK AND GEORGE

ollywood has always been criticized for its lack of values, but throughout history, you can find examples of solid relationships there, just as you can anywhere else. Take George Burns, for example. He was married for thirty-eight years to Gracie Allen until her death in 1964. And he maintained a great life-long friendship with fellow comedian Jack Benny. They went through a lot together. After Jack's death in 1976, George characterized their relationship this way: "Jack and I had a wonderful friendship for nearly fifty-five years," Burns said. "Jack never walked out on me while I sang a song, and I never walked out on him while he played the violin. We laughed together, we played together, we worked together, we ate together. I suppose that for many of those years we talked every single day."

A friendship that lasted more than half a century—wow! I hope that when I die, I'll have been that kind of friend to at least one person. I hope you'll have been too.

*The glory of friendship is not
in the outstretched hand, nor the kindly smile,
nor the joy of companionship;
it is in the spiritual inspiration that comes to
one when he discovers that someone else
believes in him and is willing to trust him.*

RALPH WALDO EMERSON

*Promises may get friends
but 'tis performance that keeps them.*

BENJAMIN FRANKLIN

The Highest Compliment

Honor God by accepting each other,
as Christ has accepted you.

Romans 15:7 (CEV)

How can you show gratitude to someone
who knows everything about you—your
failures, foibles, and darkest moments—
and still loves and accepts you whole-
heartedly? In your own small way,
imitate him by loving your friend despite
his faults. When you do, everyone wins.

Imitating Christ
is opening the door to friendship.

Billy Graham

A
BEST FRIEND

*My best friend is the
one who brings out the best in me.*

HENRY FORD

Tell me whom you frequent,
and I will tell you who you are.

FRENCH PROVERB

I Just Called to Say...

It was just a small thing, but it meant every-thing in the world to Tricia. She was in a terrible bind. She had two huge final exams in the morning—her last two—but she had fallen so far behind that she hadn't been able to study for them. The amount of material was massive, and she couldn't afford not to do well on them. So she had only one choice: As exhausted as she already was, she had to pull an all-nighter.

Tricia was "neck deep" in books when the phone rang at midnight. It was Gina. When Tricia lived in California before college, Gina had been her best friend and confidant. Even though Tricia now lived and went to school in Indiana, they still talked weekly. This night Tricia poured out her frustration to her friend, and when they finished talking, she went back to work.

She was surprised when the phone rang again an hour later. It was Gina again, calling to cheer her on and make sure she was still awake. In fact, Gina called her every hour—all night long.

As the evening wore on, Tricia kept going, encouraged by the thought that her friend would soon be calling. Then, when exam time rolled around, Tricia was ready.

There wasn't much Gina could do for Tricia that night—except encourage her, and she did just that. Knowing that someone cared helped carry Tricia through the night. Who else but a best friend, on the other side of the country, would stay up all night—just because she cared?

I praise loudly. I blame softly.
CATHERINE THE GREAT OF RUSSIA

A Boy's Best Friend

A little boy in Rochester, New York, wrote his first essay on friendship about his meaningful relationship with his dog. He turned in the following paper to his teacher.

What My Dog Means to Me

My dog means somebody nice and quiet to be with.
He does not say DO, like my mother.
He does not say DON'T, like my father.
He does not say STOP, like my big brother.
My dog Spot and I just sit quietly together,
and I like him and he likes me.
(And that's why he's my best friend.)

YOU CAN COUNT ON ME

*It makes me really glad to know
that I can depend on you.*

2 CORINTHIANS 7:16 (CEV)

People's confidence in you springs from
two things. The first is the trustworthiness
of your character. The second is how
responsible you are. The friends who
trust you do so because they can count
on you.

There can be no friendship where
there is no freedom.
Friendship loves a free air,
and will not be fenced up in straight
and narrow enclosures.

WILLIAM PENN

Defining Friends

Some folks in a small-group Bible study discussed the characteristics of good friendships, and each person contributed an idea. They came up with the following statements.

A friend is someone who sees me at my worst but never forgets my best.

A friend is someone who thinks I'm a little bit more wonderful than I really am.

A friend is someone I can talk with for hours or be with in complete silence.

A friend is a person who is as happy for my successes as I am.

A friend trusts me enough to say what he really means when talking to me.

A friend doesn't try to know more, act smarter, or be my constant teacher. A friend is a friend.

A friend is a person who listens to me even when she isn't particularly interested in what I'm saying. She listens because she sees it's important to me.

Your companions are like the buttons
on an elevator. They will either take you up,
or they will take you down.

UNKNOWN

No medicine is more valuable,
none more efficacious, none better suited
to the cure of all our temporal ills than a friend
to whom we may turn for consolation in
time of trouble, and with whom
we may share our happiness in time of joy.

GEOFFREY CHAUCER

THEIR DAY IN COURT

ne of the toughest tests for parents is standing by and watching their child make poor choices. Even harder is seeing him reap the consequences of those damaging decisions. Sometimes the only thing that keeps parents hoping and believing is the love and support of friends.

That was the case for Richard and Denise. Soon after their son Jeremy graduated from high school and enlisted in the military, he began experimenting with drugs. Jeremy had been brought up to live by the high standards of integrity and self-respect, so his flirtation was brief. He quickly vowed to never to do it again. But the story doesn't end there. During a routine investigation, Jeremy was asked by his commanding officer whether he had ever used drugs while in the army. Since Jeremy had recommitted himself to living a life of integrity, he knew he had to tell the truth. As a result of his confession, he was arrested, the only evidence to his crime being his own admission of guilt.

Jeremy's decision put Richard and Denise into great turmoil. On the one hand, they were proud that he told the truth. Richard was a pastor and celebrated Jeremy's return to his strongly held values. But at the same time, he and Denise dreaded what might happen to Jeremy. Throwing them into further turmoil was their son's decision to share his confession with the church and ask for their support while he awaited trial in a military court.

Anytime the child of a pastor takes a wrong turn in life, there is a chance that the church will be hurt and its leaders will turn against the pastor. But that's not what happened to Richard and Denise. In fact, the very people who had the power to discredit and dismiss the pastor—the church's elders—came alongside the whole family to support them. During the weeks before Jeremy's hearing, the elders and their families prayed faithfully and often set their own difficulties aside to support this young soldier and his parents.

On the day before Jeremy's court date, he and his

parents drove six hours to the army base. Imagine their surprise the morning of the trial when they emerged from their hotel rooms to find that the elders and their spouses had driven all night to be there for them.

Much has happened since that day. Jeremy received a calling from God and is now a staff pastor at the church. But no amount of time will fade the gratitude he and his parents have for those six men and women who stood by Jeremy through the darkest period of his life—people who didn't condemn him when he failed but stood by him in love and responded as friends when he needed it most.

Friendship is one of the
sweetest joys of life. Many might have failed
beneath the bitterness of
their trial had they not found a friend.
CHARLES SPURGEON

MATURE LOVE

Love should always make us tell the truth.
Then we will grow in every way and be
more like Christ, the head of the body.
Christ holds it together and makes all of its
parts work perfectly, as it grows and
becomes strong because of love.

EPHESIANS 4:15–16 (CEV)

When we were toddlers, we wanted to do
everything ourselves. But as we grew, we
began to understand that we need one
another. This is the way God designed us.
Real love is born out of maturity and is the
chief ingredient in relationships that last.

Your Name Is Written...
at the Top of My List

Some friends know all about us,
And they like us just the same.
They accept us as we are,
Not asking us to change.

They never criticize us,
While listening to our views.
They stay when others leave,
And speak when some refuse.

There aren't many friends like that,
And precious few I claim.
But at the top of my list
I've proudly put your name.

Unknown

REAL FRIENDS

Real friends . . .

Help you pack boxes and move.

Let you have the last piece of pizza.

Give you a book, not just loan one.

Tell you when you have something stuck
in your teeth.

Laugh at your dumb jokes.

Let you have the center of their cinnamon roll.

Give you a mint for your bad breath.

Put gas in your car after they borrow it.

Don't criticize your kids when you're not around.

Never sweat the small stuff.

Whose real friend are you?

*May the roof above
us never fall in—May the friends
gathered below never fall out.*

IRISH PRAYER

*Friendship with oneself is all-important,
because without it one cannot be
friends with anyone else in the world.*

ELEANOR ROOSEVELT

Undivided Attention

*My dear friends, you should be quick to
listen and slow to speak or to get angry.
If you are angry, you cannot do any of the
good things that God wants done.*

JAMES 1:19–20 (CEV)

Sometimes the greatest gift you can give
a friend is your ear. Be quiet. Listen to
the whole story. Hear with your heart.
You don't need to say a word. Just being
there will be enough.

*The greatest gift you can give another is
the purity of your attention.*

RICHARD MOSS

The Illogical Nature
of Friendship

Friendship is based on what it gives,
not what it gets.
Friendship stays alive by serving the other,
not seeking to be served.
Friendship is motivated by love, not debt.
Friendship is willing to sacrifice
without seeing or expecting a return.
It doesn't make sense, but the more it gives up,
the stronger it gets.

A true friend unbosoms freely,
advises justly, assists readily, adventures boldly,
takes all patiently, defends courageously,
and continues a friend unchangeably.

WILLIAM PENN

Being a Friend,
Even When It Isn't Easy

former coach of the Boston Celtics who led the team to two NBA championships in the 1980s, K. C. Jones had a practice of encouraging players anytime they missed what would have been the winning shot in a tough loss. He was the first person to walk over, pat the guy on back, and say, "Don't worry, we'll get 'em next time." But Jones never paid much attention to a player who did something great, which piqued the curiosity of Celtic player Kevin McHale. One day he asked Jones about it.

"Kevin," Jones replied, "after you've made the winning basket, you've got fifteen thousand people cheering for you, TV stations coming at you, and everybody giving you 'high-fives.' You don't need me then. You need a real friend when you feel that nobody likes you."

Jones was there for his players in those times of defeat and discouragement, which is one of the things that made Jones not only a great coach, but also a real friend.

A friend is someone who knows you well and still likes you.

CHEERFUL LABOR

*That's why you must encourage and help
each other, just as you are already doing.*

1 THESSALONIANS 5:11 (CEV)

Some of the best ways to encourage friends
are writing a heartfelt note or just calling
to say how much you care. The road to
friendship is paved with small kindnesses.

*If a man does not make new acquaintances
as he advances through life, he will soon
find himself left alone; A man, sir, should
keep his friendship in a constant repair.*

SAMUEL JOHNSON

A FRIENDSHIP PRAYER

Dear Lord,

Thank you for a special gift, one that
cannot be bought for any amount of money.
Thank you for a gift wrapped in beauty,
that is wonderful in all seasons and times.
Thank you for a gift that is always near in
times of need and brings great joy.
Thank you for the gift that sparkles with
freshness every day. Thank you for my friend.
May I never take this gift for granted.
Amen.

LOUDER THAN WORDS

My little children, let us not love in word or in tongue, but in deed and in truth.

1 JOHN 3:18 (NKJV)

Talking about friendship is easy. Carrying it out is harder. Your actions should speak so loudly that people cannot hear your words. If you want others to value your friendship, live it out every day.

You can make more friends in two months by becoming more interested in other people than you can in two years by trying to get people interested in you.

DALE CARNEGIE

*Friendship is the expressible
comfort of feeling safe with a person,
having neither to weigh thoughts
nor measure words.*

DINAH MARIA MULOCK CRAIK

*The supreme happiness of life
is the conviction of being loved for yourself,
or, more correctly,
being loved in spite of yourself.*

VICTOR HUGO

HOW *NOT* TO HAVE A FRIEND

Friendships fail when . . .

Communication is unclear.

Truth is violated.

Integrity is forsaken.

Time isn't invested.

Risks aren't taken.

Control is the goal.

Trust is broken.

Self-interest is the rule.

Manipulation is allowed.

God is ignored.

The better part of one's
life consists of his friendships.

ABRAHAM LINCOLN

THE GOOD WORD
OF A FRIEND

uring the Civil War, President Lincoln received many requests for pardons for soldiers who were sentenced to die for desertion. Each appeal was frequently accompanied by numerous testimonial letters from friends and powerful people.

One day the president received an appeal for a pardon that stood out among the rest. It arrived without any documents or letters vouching for the prisoner. Lincoln was puzzled by this and asked the officer in charge whether the soldier had anyone to speak on his behalf. To Lincoln's amazement the officer on duty said that the soldier had not one friend and that his entire family had been killed in the war. The president turned this over in his mind and informed the officer that he would give his ruling in the morning.

Lincoln wrestled with the issue all night. Desertion was no small matter. Overruling a death sentence would send the wrong message to other soldiers. Yet he found it difficult not to have sympathy for someone so alone in the world.

In the morning when the officer asked the president for his decision, he was shocked to hear Lincoln say that the testimony of a friend had sealed his decision on the soldier in question. When the officer reminded the president that the request had come with no letters of reference, Lincoln simply stated, "I will be his friend." He then signed the request and pardoned the man.

GOING FOR SECOND PLACE

And He sat down, called the twelve,
and said to them,
"If anyone desires to be first, he shall
be last of all and servant of all."

MARK 9:35 (NKJV)

Everyone wants to stand out from the crowd. That's just human. But your motive is the key. If you are not willing to be last, then you are not worthy to be first. If you really want to stand out, serve others. And you can start by helping a friend.

*The happiest business in all
the world is that of making friends; and no
investment on the street pays larger dividends,
for life is more than stocks and bonds,
and love than rate percent, and he who gives in
friendship's name shall reap what he has spent.*

ANNE S. EATON

HE MADE THE
NEIGHBORHOOD
WHAT IT WAS

e had been a fixture in the neighborhood for forty years. He loved it there. Even more, he loved his neighbors. But no one truly realized the depth of Bob's love until he died of colon cancer in his early seventies.

The memorial service for Bob was packed. And that's where his neighbors, many of whom knew Bob but not each other, discovered what Bob really meant to all of them.

"Bob was in charge of the neighborhood—in a good way," said Sally, "not just in the sense of being a neighborhood leader, but more like he was responsible for looking after all of us."

Michael and Trina said, "Bob was our communication link. He was the one who would check in just to be sure everything was okay, and he'd bring news of how the other neighbors were doing. He really cared about the lives of his friends and was willing to give help or moral support, or just provide friendly conversation."

Whenever they needed help, Bob would be the first person everyone turned to. He did lots of little things, like helping a couple find Prissy, their beloved Persian cat. He continually helped Mrs. Tammal by fixing her leaky faucet. (She was in her eighties, and sometimes the repair consisted of Bob simply turning off the faucet.) But there were bigger things too, such as the time when old Mr. Bonner took sick and could no longer pay rent, as low as it was. Bob dipped into his savings and paid the rent for three months while the older man got back on his feet.

"Bob's passing will leave a big void in our lives," said Richard. "We will dearly miss one of the best friends we've ever known."

WORKING IN PAIRS

*If you fall, your friend can help you up.
But if you fall without having a friend
nearby, you are really in trouble.*

ECCLESIASTES 4:10 (CEV)

Two are stronger than one. And two committed to one another are stronger than ten. We all make mistakes and even fail at times. If you travel life alone, you may have trouble getting up again when you fall. But when you travel with good friends, you can be sure that when you can't get up, someone will be there to help you.

No soul is desolate as long as
there is a human being for whom it can
feel trust and reverence.

GEORGE ELIOT

WWJD?

Do you complain when your friends let you down? When they're late to pick you up for an important engagement or don't tell you the truth? Do you keep score—about gift-giving, initiating phone calls, or picking up the tab? Are there times when you feel you give more than you get?

Jesus experienced all these things and more. His closest and most beloved friends let him down. They were unreliable and immature. They learned slowly, always the hard way. Some even betrayed him. Yet he forgave them and loved them anyway. Jesus loved his friends, but not because they were worthy of love. His love *made* them worthy.

J. I. Packer expresses this idea in his book *Knowing God:* "There is tremendous relief in knowing that His love to me is utterly realistic, based at every point on prior knowledge of the worst about me, so that no discovery now can disillusion Him about me, in the way I am so often disillusioned about myself, and quench His determination to bless me. There is, certainly, great cause for humility in the thought that He sees all the twisted things about me that my fellow men do not see . . . and that He sees more corruption in me than that which I see in myself. He wants me as His friend, and desires to be my friend, and has given His Son to die for me in order to realize this purpose."

So the next time your friends let you down, remember God's grace, use His Son as your model, and ask, "What would Jesus do?"

How to Pray as a
Friend of God

Pray for those who don't believe.

Pray for the world to be reached.

Pray for God's will to be done

on earth as in heaven.

Pray for God's kingdom to prevail.

Pray for forgiveness and grace to abound.

Pray for sick, needy, and broken people.

Pray for children.

Pray to resist temptation and evil.

Pray for God to be glorified.

A Faithful Friend

*A faithful friend is a secure shelter;
whoever finds one has found a treasure.*

THE APOCRYPHA

SHOULDERS TO LEAN ON

Bear one another's burdens,
and so fulfill the law of Christ.
GALATIANS 6:2 (NKJV)

A real friend notices when you are bent
under the weight of a great burden,
and without saying a word, simply steps
alongside you to help carry it. With the
help of a friend, you can endure
almost anything.

A friend should bear his friend's infirmities.
WILLIAM SHAKESPEARE

An Old Friend...
and a New One

hen I first met Janene, she and her best friend Savannah were inseparable. One of the most vibrant people I've ever met, Janene is a classy artist and talented entrepreneur. She has a passion for life, her emotions heaped like paint on an artist's palate, the colors sparkling with pleasure and joy. To be a friend of Janene is to be loved well.

That was also especially true of Savannah. She was regal, striking, tall, and beautiful with honey-colored hair. She was fun loving and graceful, and she drooled a lot. You see, Savannah was a Great Dane.

Janene and Savannah had a close relationship. They often went for walks together and played by the poolside, but most of the time, it was enough for them just to be together. For years, if you saw Janene, you saw Savannah alongside her.

Then one day Janene noticed that Savannah wasn't her old self. She seemed to mope around a lot. That's when Janene realized that her faithful canine friend was in pain. When she took the dog to the veterinarian, she was horrified to hear that nothing could be done. Janene had two choices: to let Savannah keep suffering great pain or to "put her down."

Janene was numb as she drove home. She knew she couldn't allow Savannah to live in pain, so she knew what she had to do. She couldn't bear the thought of watching her dog die, but neither could she envision her beloved Savannah being put to sleep in a frightening environment with no one who loved her. Janene was totally at a loss. Then she thought of her friend Patti. Patti was tough and self-reliant. And Janene believed she would be willing to help.

The two women tearfully packed Savannah into the car and made their way to the veterinarian's office. That's when Janene realized she had very few pictures of Savannah. They bought a disposable camera at a convenience store and drove to a nearby park. Patti snapped shots as Janene romped with Savannah and tried not to think about what was about to come.

The ride to the office seemed almost unreal, and all too soon they arrived. The doctor invited Janene, Patti, and Savannah into a back room where he gently explained what would take place. After the needle was placed in Savannah's hip, she stumbled and fell. And while Patti and Janene wept, Savannah lay her head in Janene's lap and went to sleep.

It took a very long time for Janene to recover from that experience. Even now she has days when she misses Savannah. But another significant thing happened that day. Janene and Patti could sense that a deeper bond was being forged between them. As the two women rode home in silence, Janene realized through her grief that she had indeed lost one dear friend, but in the process she had gained another.

NO GREATER LOVE

Greater love has no one than this,
than to lay down one's
life for his friends.

JOHN 15:13 (NKJV)

You may never be called upon to
make such a sacrifice for a friend, but
the question to ask yourself is this:
Am I willing?

Life is nothing without friendship.

QUINTUS ENNIUS

FRIENDSHIP IS THE FOUNDATION

"In research at our clinic, my colleagues and I have discovered that friendship is the springboard to every other love. Friendships spill over onto the other important relationships of life. People with no friends usually have a diminished capacity for sustaining any kind of love. They tend to go through a succession of marriages, be estranged from various family members, and have trouble getting along at work. On the other hand, those who learn how to love their friends tend to make long and fulfilling marriages, get along well with the people at work, and enjoy their children."

ALAN LOY MCGINNIS

FROM *THE FRIENDSHIP FACTOR*

*In friendship we find nothing false
or insincere; everything is straightforward,
and springs from the heart.*

CICERO

When Nothing Else Will Do

S haron and Dan sat huddled on the couch, each silent and hurting over what had taken place just hours before. Christmas that year had been wonderful. Sharon's prodigal daughter had returned home early that spring. Leading up to her return had been four years of upheaval and pain, but that Christmas, they were finally all united in heart.

The first few months after their daughter's return had been rocky at best. But over the course of time, Sharon and Dan began to see a change. They thought their prayers had been answered—their daughter seemed healthy, both emotionally and spiritually.

On Christmas night, their girl sat between them on the couch in front of a roaring fire. She thanked them for their love and patience, and they pledged new beginnings as laughter and hugs filled the night.

But everything took an ugly turn only two days later

when their sixteen-year-old daughter suddenly told them she wanted no part of what they had to offer. She wanted her own life. And within the hour, she was gone.

They were numb as people tried to console them. Friends, family, and their pastor all did what they could to comfort them. But nothing seemed to help. There was nothing anyone could say or do to make them feel better.

Then one day a friend named Linda called. She seemed to have very little in common with Sharon. She had never gone through anything like what Sharon was experiencing. In fact, she seemed to have a perfect daughter. But when Linda called, she offered no solutions or advice. She called and simply said, "I don't know how you feel, but if you'll let me, I'll come cry with you." And she did. It was the best thing she could have done.

Sharon's hurting heart was forever changed that day, not by a quick answer to her problem or any words of wisdom, but because she knew Linda cared. She was willing to simply cry with her. Isn't that what friendship is really all about?

Friendship in Progress

Just as iron sharpens iron, friends sharpen
the minds of each other.

PROVERBS 27:17 (CEV)

Friends challenge one another to reach
their God-given potential. This
requires spending time together and
understanding each other's dreams,
desires, and abilities. It also takes
courage. Honest communication is
essential in the process of "sharpening"
one another.

Investment Advice

Build a beautiful house; eventually it will crumble. Develop a fine career; one day you must step down. Earn huge sums of money, but you can't take it with you. Accomplish great things, and someone will eventually surpass you.

Discouraged? Please don't be. There is something you can invest in that lasts. Friendship. When you build relationships and develop people, you earn respect and accomplish something that can't be measured or bought. Friendship is the only investment that requires all you have and yet returns more than you gave. If you're looking for a great investment, give yourself to your friends.

CHRISTIAN LOVE

*Love is kind and patient,
never jealous, boastful, proud, or rude.
Love isn't selfish or quick tempered.
It doesn't keep a record of wrongs that
others do. Love rejoices in the truth,
but not in evil. Love is always supportive,
loyal, hopeful, and trusting.*

1 CORINTHIANS 13:4–7 (CEV)

Nowhere else has the essence of love
been expressed in so few words. Let
them settle into your heart—and they
will change your life.

And the song,
from beginning to end, I found in
the heart of an old friend.

HENRY WADSWORTH LONGFELLOW

UNDER THEIR WINGS

hen a young couple goes into ministry at an old established church, they often have a tough time. But Kirk and Denise were fortunate. When Kirk was twenty-three years old, he and Denise accepted the call to pastor the church where he had grown up, and they had Don and Tamara on their side.

From the start, the two couples felt a great connection. Don and Tamara, parents of three children, owned a successful business and were strong leaders in the church. They took the young pastor and his wife under their wings and shared everything they could with them. They frequently took them out to eat and watched their children so that Kirk and Denise could get out alone together. And on those tough Monday mornings when Kirk felt like he was ready to quit, Tamara would pray for him.

Don and Tamara's favorite way to help the young

couple was to invite them to their camp in the Florida everglades. The families would ride in Don and Tamara's airboat, fish on the canal banks, catch alligators, and hunt wild turkeys in the woods. For fifteen years, these friends shared every Thanksgiving together at the camp, and every year they hunted and ate the turkeys they caught.

Kirk and Denise wouldn't have made it through those difficult early years of ministry without Don and Tamara. That's why it was especially hard on them when they found out that Tamara had cancer. On their last trip together on a Labor Day weekend, Tamara coughed all night long. She thought it was just an allergy, but when she visited her doctor, he gave her only a short time to live.

During the next few months, it was Kirk and Denise's turn to reach out and take care of Don and Tamara. They did what they could. Kirk often sat with her in her living room and prayed for Tamara. Her hair was gone from chemotherapy, her weight was down, and she was ever so pale, but she never lost her tender spirit or her faith. And when she died two days before Christmas, Kirk officiated her funeral.

Kirk and Denise still think of Tamara often, especially when the wind blows through the trees late at night or when they eat turkey at Thanksgiving. They miss her, but they're grateful for the time they had with her, and the friendship that they hope to someday rekindle in heaven.

There are deep sorrows and killing cares in life, but the encouragement and love of friends were given us to make all difficulties bearable.

JOHN OLIVER HOBBES

THE EDIFICATION FACTOR

*Therefore let us pursue the things
which make for peace and the things by
which one may edify another.*

ROMANS 14:19 (NKJV)

It's easy to find fault in others. It's more
difficult to build others up. But taking
the high road instead of the low leads to
a higher level of living. If you truly love
your friends, bring out the best in them.

*Encouragement after censure
is as the sun after a shower.*

JOHANN WOLFGANG VON GOETHE

A Friend of the Truest Kind

A friend...

is someone who keeps your secrets
and never divulges them, even if tortured—
or worse, tempted with chocolate.

is someone who quietly destroys the photograph
that makes you look like a beached whale.

is someone who knows you don't know
what you're talking about, but allows you to reach
that conclusion on your own.

is someone who goes with you on a diet—
and off it too.

is someone who doesn't say, "I told you so,"
no matter how tempting it might be.

A friend of the truest kind is kind and true to you.

A "Real" Friend

"What is real?" asked the rabbit one day. "Does it mean having things that buzz inside you, and a stick out handle?"

"Real isn't how you were made," said the Skin Horse, "it's a thing that happens to you. When a child loves you for a long time, not just to play with, but really loves you, then you become Real. It doesn't happen all at once," said the Skin Horse. "You become. It takes a long time . . . Generally, by the time you are Real, most of your hair has been rubbed off and your eyes drop out and you get loose in the joints and very shabby. But these things don't matter at all, because once you are Real, you can't be ugly, except to people who don't understand."

MARGERY WILLIAMS

FROM *THE VELVETEEN RABBIT*

PROSPERITY

But do not forget to do good and to share,
for with such sacrifices God is well pleased.

HEBREWS 13:16 (NKJV)

Have you ever wondered why you have
been blessed with what you possess? The
answer is simple: to share it with others.
As you go through the day today, remember to give a little part of yourself to others.
There's no better way to bless them.

In prosperity our friends know us.
In adversity we know our friends.

UNKNOWN

I keep my friends as misers
do their treasure, because, of all the
things granted us by wisdom,
none is greater or better than friendship.

PIETRO ARETINO

A Friend Who
Refused to Give Up

hip and Darlene had been married for five years when they decided to start a family, but for over a year they were unable to conceive a child. Then on Valentine's Day, Darlene got the best news of her life: She was pregnant. That night, at their romantic dinner, they celebrated more than just the joy of their own relationship. They celebrated the new life that was on the way.

Everything progressed fine for Chip and Darlene—that is, until a drunk driver smashed his pickup truck into Darlene's car in a head-on collision. Darlene was lucky—she suffered only a broken arm, cuts, and bruises—but the baby wasn't. He didn't survive the accident. A few days later, the couple wept over the tiny casket of little Christopher, the child they never got to know.

The couple was devastated. During the next several weeks, Chip worked long hours trying to get his mind off of what had happened. Meanwhile Darlene, recovering from her injuries, had nothing but time to think. At first she just felt tired and wanted to sleep a lot. But then the emotional turmoil got worse. It became physically difficult for her to get out of bed, and she stopped taking care of herself. She ate poorly and wore dirty clothes. As Darlene's depression grew, the hurt turned to anger, and her anger turned to bitterness. She lashed out at everyone. After a while, even her closest friends stopped visiting or calling. They just couldn't stand to be around her.

But there was one person who kept coming back. Her name was Melissa. Every day for more than two months she made lunch for Darlene, talked with her, and tried to encourage her. No matter what mood Darlene was in, Melissa would not give up on her. They talked together, cried together, prayed together—and just sat quietly together for a couple of hours every day.

Things looked pretty bleak at first. But after about three months, Darlene began to show signs of recovery. Little by little she regained perspective and hope. Today, she is fully recovered, and she enjoys spending time with her twin boys who were born a year after she lost Christopher. She often wonders how Melissa was able to hang in there with her. But more than anything, she's grateful for Melissa, the friend who, she considers, saved her life.

Is any pleasure on earth as great as a circle of Christian friends by a fire?

C. S. LEWIS

Tombstone Testimonies

What will people say at your funeral? What will be the main theme of their thoughts? Will they describe you as kind and compassionate? Will they talk about missing the best friend they ever had? You may think that your eulogy is beyond your reach, but it isn't. You are writing it today—on the hearts and lives of the people around you. So don't hold back. Write it in bold strokes of love.

A person can have no better epitaph
than that which is inscribed in
the hearts of his friends.

Unknown

FAITHFUL FRIENDS

Faithful friends…

Believe in each other.

Bring out the best in each other.

Celebrate the victories.

Comfort each other during

the difficult times.

Tell the truth no matter what.

Insist on growth.

Bring honor to God.

WISE COUNSEL

*The sweet smell of incense
can make you feel good, but true
friendship is better still.*

PROVERBS 27:9 (CEV)

Wisdom is the greatest gift a friend can give you.

*No receipt openeth the heart but a
true friend, to whom you may impart griefs,
joys, fears, hopes, suspicions, counsels,
and whatsoever lieth upon the heart to oppress
it, in a kind of civil shrift or confession.*

FRANCIS BACON

BE SURE TO SAY THANKS

No matter how long you have loved your friends, no matter how deeply, always express appreciation to the special people who share pieces of their lives with you. Gratitude is one of those pure elements that make relationships deep, rich, and meaningful. Say thank you often. Be creative. And always express yourself from the heart.

*The more we love our friends,
the less we flatter them; it is by excusing
nothing that pure love shows itself.*

JEAN-BAPTISTE MOLIÈRE

Twenty-Four Carat Friendship

esse Owens seemed sure to win the long jump at the 1936 Olympic games in Berlin, Germany. Just the year before he had set three world records in a single day. In fact, he was the record holder for the running broad jump with a distance of 26 feet and 8 ¼ inches—a record that stood for 25 years.

As he walked to the long jump pit, however, Owens saw a tall, blue-eyed-blond, German gentleman taking practice jumps in the 26 feet range. Owens was nervous. He was acutely aware of the tension his presence created, knowing of the Nazis' desire to prove the so-called Aryan superiority, particularly over anyone of African descent.

The pressure was overwhelming, and on his first jump, Owens inadvertently leaped from several inches beyond the takeoff board. Rattled, he fouled on his second attempt too. He was only one foul away from being eliminated.

At this point, the tall German approached Owens. In view of the entire stadium, the white "model of Nazi manhood" stood before the black son of a sharecropper. They talked. "What were the two men saying?" everyone wondered.

The German was introducing himself. His name was Luz Long. "You should be able to qualify with your eyes closed!" he said to Owens, referring to his two earlier jumps.

Since the qualifying distance was only 23 feet and 5 ½ inches, Long suggested that Owens make a mark several inches before the takeoff board and jump from there—just to play it safe. Amazing! At the height of the Nazi era, this model of Germany's strength was providing assistance and words of encouragement to a man considered his foe both on and off the field.

As you might have imagined, Owens qualified easily. In the finals, Owens set an Olympic record and earned the second of his four gold medals at those Olympics games. And who was the first person to congratulate Owens? Luz Long—in full view of Adolf Hitler.

Owens never saw Long again. In fact, the German athlete was killed in World War II. But Jesse never forgot him.

"You could melt down all the medals and cups I have," Owens later wrote, "and they wouldn't be plating on the twenty-four carat friendship I felt for Luz Long," the man who faced the wrath of the Third Reich and Adolph Hitler himself to cross the line and extend his hand in friendship.

KEN SUTTERFIELD

ADAPTED FROM *THE POWER OF AN ENCOURAGING WORD*

Our Best Friend

The Old Testament says that Abraham and Moses were called friends of God. In the New Testament, Jesus teaches that friendship with God is not reserved for the elite, the chosen, or the few. Anyone who follows Christ, obeys His commands, and loves others can be His friend.

Jesus said, "No longer do I call you servants . . . but I have called you friends."

JOHN 15:15 (NKJV)

ACKNOWLEDGEMENTS

*Grateful acknowledgement is made to the following publishers
for permission to reprint copyrighted material.*

Alan Loy McGinnis, *The Friendship Factor.* ©1979 Augsburg Publishing
House. Used by permission of Augsburg Fortress.

J. I. Packer, *Knowing God.* Downers Grove, Ill.:
InterVarsity Press, 1993.

Ken Sutterfield, *The Power of an Encouraging Word.*
Green Forest, Ariz.: New Leaf Press, 1997.